Note 2 Self

Daily Inspiration, Mediations & Affirmations
To Accompany You On Your Life's Journey

Volume 1

Keisha A. Rivers-Shorty

ISBN-10: 1480197483
ISBN-13: 978-1480197480

DEDICATION

This book is dedicated to those who counseled me,
supported me, taught me, encouraged me, shunned me,
laughed at me, mocked me, befriended me, protected me,
abandoned me, hated me and loved me. Because of your
presence, I have experienced a lot; learned much and
changed greatly.

It is presented as a gift to those who are embarking on
their journey and need the encouragement to take the first
(of many) steps.

You are more than enough.
Live. Laugh. Love.

~Keisha

KEISHA A. RIVERS-SHORTY

ACKNOWLEDGMENTS
&
SPECIAL THANKS

A very special thanks to the people in my life who have stood by me regardless of the incompleteness of who I was at any given moment and have loved me as I have always been because they could see who I was always destined to become.

To Earl--you have been my greatest challenge, my biggest supporter and my best friend. The lessons I have learned and the person I have become are due in large part to the life we shared. Thank you.

To my mom, Katie--thank you for believing in me & loving me regardless.

To my "other" parents, Harriet & "Dude"—may you rest in peace and know that your "Princess" finally did it. I love you always.

To Richard—thank you for being a true friend, supporter and confidant, and for giving me the courage to finally step out and be the person that you saw I could be.

There are others who have taught me much and supported me through it all. I cannot list you all here, but know that you are appreciated and you are loved.

~Keisha

KEISHA A. RIVERS-SHORTY

A MESSAGE FROM THE AUTHOR

Congratulations on undertaking this journey! I compiled "Note 2 Self" from a collection of daily inspirational messages, insights and reminders that I've created over the years to help me get through the journey of each day. Sometimes the messages are inspirational, sometimes enlightening; but always they represent an "ah-ha' moment that I've experienced during my daily journey to "be" and to "become".

I am not finished with my journey—nor am I done learning, discovering, being and becoming.

I share these in the hopes that I can help someone else who maybe doesn't have that inner (or outer) voice speaking to them, encouraging them, challenging them and supporting them through their journey.

I was fortunate at some points to have others to help guide me. Now I want to return the favor.

When you read each "Note 2 Self", say it in your head or say it out loud. But either way, hear the words in YOUR voice as you have a conversation with yourself.

~Keisha

HOW TO USE THIS BOOK

Organized as a series of 90 Day "Conversations" that you have with your "Self", "NOTE 2 SELF" features a daily note, message or reminder for you read and then engage in a three-step process:

1) *Reflect*—You are to think about and reflect on the message for that day. What does it mean to you?
2) *Relate*—How does this connect or resonate with you? What circumstances or experiences have you had that relate to this message?
3) *Release Yourself to Take Action*—What will you do and how will you release yourself to take action based on today's message?

"NOTE 2 SELF" is designed as a companion to the KARS "Release Yourself Series"™ as part of the KARS Paperback Coaching Program™ and has been created as a way of guiding you as you begin the process of self-discovery, self-determination and self-actualization.

You begin on Day 1 and progress through each day's message in order. Consider this an independent, self-study where you are getting to really think about who you are, what you want and where you're going in life.

To that end, it is recommended that you keep an additional journal during this process so that you can have more space to record your thoughts, feelings, ideas, responses to the questions posed and questions of your own.

It doesn't matter what day of the week, month or year you get this book and get started. The day you begin the process is DAY ONE for you.

Now, I know you're probably wondering-- "Why 90 days?" 90 days is more or less three months—which is, in the natural order of things—the usual length of a season within a year. Each time you take a journey to make a change in your life, you're embarking on a new "season" of Challenge, Change and Choice.

As a result, we're going to Challenge your assumptions; Change your thinking and encourage you to make a Choice about what you're going to do to get what you want and create the life you were destined to have.

There will be subsequent "Note 2 Self" Volumes to follow that take you through the next" Seasons" in your life's journey.

Along the way, with purchase of this book, you're automatically entitled to participate in The KARS Book Club where you'll receive access to bi-weekly conference calls that allow you to engage in the process of and connect with others who are traveling along the journey just as you are. You'll receive affirmation, motivation and inspiration through your connections via phone and will also have the opportunity to participate in an online discussion group.

Feel free to join the conversation during any time in your journey. It doesn't matter which day you're currently reading or which volume of the Series. The important part is the process, the collaboration and the reflection on both the process and your practice as you have the conversations you need to have in order to do the things you want to do and become who you want to and were destined to be.

You're not in it alone.

Now. Ready. Set.
Let's GO!

KEISHA A. RIVERS-SHORTY

THE JOURNEY BEGINS...

DAY 1

Note 2 Self: "Some lessons cannot be taught. They must be lived to be understood."

1) *Reflect*: What do you believe this means? What does it say to you?

_____
_____
_____
_____
_____
_____

2) *Relate*: How does this connect with your life/experiences? Describe a memory, experience or feeling that you've had as a result of this note.

_____
_____
_____
_____
_____
_____
_____

3) *Release Yourself*: What actions will you release yourself to take in your life as a result of today's note?

_____
_____
_____
_____
_____
_____
_____

4) Your Own Notes, Questions, Thoughts, Musings

DAY 2

Note 2 Self: "The longest journey begins with the first step. No matter how insurmountable or impossible it may seem, ultimately you get to your goal by just doing something—anything—a little at a time."

1) *Reflect*: What do you believe this means? What does it say to you?

_____
_____
_____
_____
_____

2) *Relate*: How does this connect with your life/experiences? Describe a memory, experience or feeling that you've had as a result of this note.

_____
_____
_____
_____
_____

3) *Release Yourself*: What actions will you release yourself to take in your life as a result of today's note?

_____
_____
_____
_____
_____
_____
_____

4) *Your Own Notes, Questions, Thoughts, Musings*

_____

_____

_____

_____

_____

_____

_____

_____

_____

_____

_____

_____

_____

_____

_____

_____

_____

_____

_____

_____

_____

_____

_____

_____

_____

_____

_____

_____

_____

_____

_____

_____

_____

_____

DAY 3

Note 2 Self: **"Life is a teachable moment. What have you learned today?"**

1) *Reflect*: What do you believe this means? What does it say to you?

_____

_____

_____

_____

_____

_____

2) *Relate*: How does this connect with your life/experiences? Describe a memory, experience or feeling that you've had as a result of this note.

_____

_____

_____

_____

_____

3) *Release Yourself*: What actions will you release yourself to take in your life as a result of today's note?

_____

_____

_____

_____

_____

_____

_____

4) *Your Own Notes, Questions, Thoughts, Musings*

_____

_____

_____

_____

_____

_____

_____

_____

_____

_____

_____

_____

_____

_____

_____

_____

_____

_____

_____

_____

_____

_____

_____

_____

_____

_____

_____

_____

_____

_____

DAY 4

Note 2 Self: "The only person you should worry about proving things to is yourself."

1) *Reflect*: What do you believe this means? What does it say to you?

_____

_____

_____

_____

_____

_____

_____

2) *Relate*: How does this connect with your life/experiences? Describe a memory, experience or feeling that you've had as a result of this note.

_____

_____

_____

_____

_____

_____

_____

3) *Release Yourself*: What actions will you release yourself to take in your life as a result of today's note?

_____

_____

_____

_____

_____

_____

_____

4) *Your Own Notes, Questions, Thoughts, Musings*

DAY 5

Note 2 Self: "See the possibilities in the uncertainty."

1) **Reflect**: What do you believe this means? What does it say to you?

_____

_____

_____

_____

_____

_____

_____

2) **Relate**: How does this connect with your life/experiences? Describe a memory, experience or feeling that you've had as a result of this note.

_____

_____

_____

_____

_____

_____

_____

3) **Release Yourself**: What actions will you release yourself to take in your life as a result of today's note?

_____

_____

_____

_____

_____

_____

_____

4) *Your Own Notes, Questions, Thoughts, Musings*

_____

_____

_____

_____

_____

_____

_____

_____

_____

_____

_____

_____

_____

_____

_____

_____

_____

_____

_____

_____

_____

_____

_____

_____

_____

_____

_____

DAY 6

Note 2 Self: "Give yourself permission—to succeed, to fail, to learn, to wonder, to do—to BE."

1) *Reflect*: What do you believe this means? What does it say to you?

_____

_____

_____

_____

_____

_____

_____

2) *Relate*: How does this connect with your life/experiences? Describe a memory, experience or feeling that you've had as a result of this note.

_____

_____

_____

_____

_____

_____

3) *Release Yourself*: What actions will you release yourself to take in your life as a result of today's note?

_____

_____

_____

_____

_____

_____

_____

4) *Your Own Notes, Questions, Thoughts, Musings*

_____

_____

_____

_____

_____

_____

_____

_____

_____

_____

_____

_____

_____

_____

_____

_____

_____

_____

_____

_____

_____

_____

_____

_____

_____

_____

_____

_____

DAY 7

Note 2 Self: "Your choices reflect not only who you are, but what you really value."

1) *Reflect*: What do you believe this means? What does it say to you?

_____

_____

_____

_____

_____

_____

_____

2) *Relate*: How does this connect with your life/experiences? Describe a memory, experience or feeling that you've had as a result of this note.

_____

_____

_____

_____

_____

_____

_____

3) *Release Yourself*: What actions will you release yourself to take in your life as a result of today's note?

_____

_____

_____

_____

_____

_____

_____

4) *Your Own Notes, Questions, Thoughts, Musings*

_____

_____

_____

_____

_____

_____

_____

_____

_____

_____

_____

_____

_____

_____

_____

_____

_____

_____

_____

_____

_____

_____

_____

_____

_____

DAY 8

Note 2 Self: "Your words paint a picture of who you are. Choose them carefully."

1) *Reflect*: What do you believe this means? What does it say to you?

_____

_____

_____

_____

_____

_____

_____

2) *Relate*: How does this connect with your life/experiences? Describe a memory, experience or feeling that you've had as a result of this note.

_____

_____

_____

_____

_____

_____

_____

3) *Release Yourself*: What actions will you release yourself to take in your life as a result of today's note?

_____

_____

_____

_____

_____

_____

_____

4) *Your Own Notes, Questions, Thoughts, Musings*

_____

_____

_____

_____

_____

_____

_____

_____

_____

_____

_____

_____

_____

_____

_____

_____

_____

_____

_____

_____

_____

_____

_____

_____

_____

DAY 9

Note 2 Self: *"Live each moment, savor each experience and embrace each encounter with the wonderment of it being your first time and the appreciation that it might be your last."*

1) ***Reflect***: What do you believe this means? What does it say to you?

_____
_____
_____
_____
_____
_____

2) ***Relate***: How does this connect with your life/experiences? Describe a memory, experience or feeling that you've had as a result of this note.

_____
_____
_____
_____
_____
_____

3) ***Release Yourself:*** What actions will you release yourself to take in your life as a result of today's note?

_____
_____
_____
_____
_____
_____

4) *Your Own Notes, Questions, Thoughts, Musings*

_____

_____

_____

_____

_____

_____

_____

_____

_____

_____

_____

_____

_____

_____

_____

_____

_____

_____

_____

_____

_____

_____

_____

_____

_____

DAY 10

Note 2 Self: "Removing people from aspects of your life is not "punishing" them; it's protecting and valuing you."

1) **Reflect**: What do you believe this means? What does it say to you?

_____
_____
_____
_____
_____
_____
_____

2) **Relate**: How does this connect with your life/experiences? Describe a memory, experience or feeling that you've had as a result of this note.

_____
_____
_____
_____
_____
_____

3) **Release Yourself**: What actions will you release yourself to take in your life as a result of today's note?

_____
_____
_____
_____
_____
_____

4) *Your Own Notes, Questions, Thoughts, Musings*

_____

_____

_____

_____

_____

_____

_____

_____

_____

_____

_____

_____

_____

_____

_____

_____

_____

_____

_____

_____

_____

_____

_____

DAY 11

Note 2 Self: *"Whenever you think about going back to an old situation—remember you left it behind for a reason."*

1) *Reflect*: What do you believe this means? What does it say to you?

_____

_____

_____

_____

_____

_____

2) *Relate*: How does this connect with your life/experiences? Describe a memory, experience or feeling that you've had as a result of this note.

_____

_____

_____

_____

_____

_____

_____

3) *Release Yourself*: What actions will you release yourself to take in your life as a result of today's note?

_____

_____

_____

_____

_____

_____

_____

4) *Your Own Notes, Questions, Thoughts, Musings*

_____

_____

_____

_____

_____

_____

_____

_____

_____

_____

_____

_____

_____

_____

_____

_____

_____

_____

_____

_____

_____

_____

_____

_____

_____

_____

DAY 12

Note 2 Self: *"When you tap into the vision of who you are created to be, then you can step into the life you are destined to live."*

1) **Reflect**: What do you believe this means? What does it say to you?

_____

_____

_____

_____

_____

_____

_____

2) **Relate**: How does this connect with your life/experiences? Describe a memory, experience or feeling that you've had as a result of this note.

_____

_____

_____

_____

_____

_____

3) **Release Yourself**: What actions will you release yourself to take in your life as a result of today's note?

_____

_____

_____

_____

_____

_____

4) *Your Own Notes, Questions, Thoughts, Musings*

_____

_____

_____

_____

_____

_____

_____

_____

_____

_____

_____

_____

_____

_____

_____

_____

_____

_____

_____

_____

_____

_____

_____

_____

_____

_____

_____

_____

DAY 13

Note 2 Self: "The only "perfect" time to do anything is once you've made up your mind to do it."

1) *Reflect*: What do you believe this means? What does it say to you?

_____

_____

_____

_____

_____

_____

_____

2) *Relate*: How does this connect with your life/experiences? Describe a memory, experience or feeling that you've had as a result of this note.

_____

_____

_____

_____

_____

_____

3) *Release Yourself*: What actions will you release yourself to take in your life as a result of today's note?

_____

_____

_____

_____

_____

_____

_____

4) *Your Own Notes, Questions, Thoughts, Musings*

_____

_____

_____

_____

_____

_____

_____

_____

_____

_____

_____

_____

_____

_____

_____

_____

_____

_____

_____

_____

_____

_____

_____

_____

_____

DAY 14

Note 2 Self: "You can only be intimidated when you don't know and value who you are."

1) **Reflect**: What do you believe this means? What does it say to you?

_____

_____

_____

_____

_____

_____

_____

2) **Relate**: How does this connect with your life/experiences? Describe a memory, experience or feeling that you've had as a result of this note.

_____

_____

_____

_____

_____

_____

3) **Release Yourself:** What actions will you release yourself to take in your life as a result of today's note?

_____

_____

_____

_____

_____

_____

_____

4) *Your Own Notes, Questions, Thoughts, Musings*

_____

_____

_____

_____

_____

_____

_____

_____

_____

_____

_____

_____

_____

_____

_____

_____

_____

_____

_____

_____

_____

_____

_____

_____

_____

DAY 15

Note 2 Self: **"You are more than the sum of your circumstances."**

1) **Reflect**: What do you believe this means? What does it say to you?

_____

_____

_____

_____

_____

_____

2) **Relate**: How does this connect with your life/experiences? Describe a memory, experience or feeling that you've had as a result of this note.

_____

_____

_____

_____

_____

3) **Release Yourself**: What actions will you release yourself to take in your life as a result of today's note?

_____

_____

_____

_____

_____

_____

_____

4) *Your Own Notes, Questions, Thoughts, Musings*

_____

_____

_____

_____

_____

_____

_____

_____

_____

_____

_____

_____

_____

_____

_____

_____

_____

_____

_____

_____

_____

_____

_____

_____

_____

_____

DAY 16

Note 2 Self: "If you're constantly 'Responding/Reacting'; you're not 'Creating/Acting'."

1) *Reflect*: What do you believe this means? What does it say to you?

_____
_____
_____
_____
_____
_____
_____

2) *Relate*: How does this connect with your life/experiences? Describe a memory, experience or feeling that you've had as a result of this note.

_____
_____
_____
_____
_____
_____

3) *Release Yourself*: What actions will you release yourself to take in your life as a result of today's note?

_____
_____
_____
_____
_____
_____

4) *Your Own Notes, Questions, Thoughts, Musings*

_____

_____

_____

_____

_____

_____

_____

_____

_____

_____

_____

_____

_____

_____

_____

_____

_____

_____

_____

_____

_____

_____

_____

_____

DAY 17

Note 2 Self: "Ultimately everything is a choice."

1) **Reflect**: What do you believe this means? What does it say to you?

   _____

   _____

   _____

   _____

   _____

   _____

   _____

2) **Relate**: How does this connect with your life/experiences? Describe a memory, experience or feeling that you've had as a result of this note.

   _____

   _____

   _____

   _____

   _____

   _____

3) **Release Yourself**: What actions will you release yourself to take in your life as a result of today's note?

   _____

   _____

   _____

   _____

   _____

   _____

   _____

4) *Your Own Notes, Questions, Thoughts, Musings*

_____

_____

_____

_____

_____

_____

_____

_____

_____

_____

_____

_____

_____

_____

_____

_____

_____

_____

_____

_____

_____

_____

_____

_____

_____

DAY 18

Note 2 Self: "Whatever obstacle is facing you—embrace it, use it and rise above it. Take the next step higher to get even closer to the vision, the dream and the true reality of who you are destined to be."

1) **Reflect**: What do you believe this means? What does it say to you?

_____
_____
_____
_____
_____
_____

2) **Relate**: How does this connect with your life/experiences? Describe a memory, experience or feeling that you've had as a result of this note.

_____
_____
_____
_____
_____

3) **Release Yourself**: What actions will you release yourself to take in your life as a result of today's note?

_____
_____
_____
_____
_____
_____

4) *Your Own Notes, Questions, Thoughts, Musings*

_____

_____

_____

_____

_____

_____

_____

_____

_____

_____

_____

_____

_____

_____

_____

_____

_____

_____

_____

_____

_____

_____

_____

_____

_____

_____

_____

DAY 19

Note 2 Self: *"You must invest in yourself if you expect others to invest in you."*

1) *Reflect*: What do you believe this means? What does it say to you?

_____

_____

_____

_____

_____

_____

_____

2) *Relate*: How does this connect with your life/experiences? Describe a memory, experience or feeling that you've had as a result of this note.

_____

_____

_____

_____

_____

3) *Release Yourself*: What actions will you release yourself to take in your life as a result of today's note?

_____

_____

_____

_____

_____

_____

_____

4) *Your Own Notes, Questions, Thoughts, Musings*

_____

_____

_____

_____

_____

_____

_____

_____

_____

_____

_____

_____

_____

_____

_____

_____

_____

_____

_____

_____

_____

_____

_____

_____

_____

DAY 20

Note 2 Self: "Yes, everything happens for a reason; and it's usually because of the choices you make."

1) *Reflect*: What do you believe this means? What does it say to you?

_____

_____

_____

_____

_____

_____

2) *Relate*: How does this connect with your life/experiences? Describe a memory, experience or feeling that you've had as a result of this note.

_____

_____

_____

_____

_____

_____

3) *Release Yourself*: What actions will you release yourself to take in your life as a result of today's note?

_____

_____

_____

_____

_____

_____

4) *Your Own Notes, Questions, Thoughts, Musings*

_____

_____

_____

_____

_____

_____

_____

_____

_____

_____

_____

_____

_____

_____

_____

_____

_____

_____

_____

_____

_____

_____

_____

_____

_____

DAY 21

Note 2 Self: "The only thing promised about your life is that you will be the one living it."

1) ***Reflect***: What do you believe this means? What does it say to you?

_____

_____

_____

_____

_____

_____

_____

2) ***Relate***: How does this connect with your life/experiences? Describe a memory, experience or feeling that you've had as a result of this note.

_____

_____

_____

_____

_____

_____

3) ***Release Yourself***: What actions will you release yourself to take in your life as a result of today's note?

_____

_____

_____

_____

_____

_____

_____

4) Your Own Notes, Questions, Thoughts, Musings

_____

_____

_____

_____

_____

_____

_____

_____

_____

_____

_____

_____

_____

_____

_____

_____

_____

_____

_____

_____

_____

_____

_____

_____

DAY 22

Note 2 Self: "Take inspiration from others'
triumphs; motivation from others' perseverance
and lessons from others' mistakes."

1) *Reflect*: What do you believe this means? What does it
say to you?

_____

_____

_____

_____

_____

_____

_____

2) *Relate*: How does this connect with your
life/experiences? Describe a memory, experience or
feeling that you've had as a result of this note.

_____

_____

_____

_____

_____

_____

3) *Release Yourself*: What actions will you release
yourself to take in your life as a result of today's note?

_____

_____

_____

_____

_____

_____

_____

4) *Your Own Notes, Questions, Thoughts, Musings*

_____

_____

_____

_____

_____

_____

_____

_____

_____

_____

_____

_____

_____

_____

_____

_____

_____

_____

_____

_____

_____

_____

_____

_____

_____

DAY 23

Note 2 Self: ***"If you don't believe you're worth it, no one else will either."***

1) ***Reflect:*** What do you believe this means? What does it say to you?

_____

_____

_____

_____

_____

_____

_____

2) ***Relate:*** How does this connect with your life/experiences? Describe a memory, experience or feeling that you've had as a result of this note.

_____

_____

_____

_____

_____

_____

3) ***Release Yourself:*** What actions will you release yourself to take in your life as a result of today's note?

_____

_____

_____

_____

_____

_____

_____

4) *Your Own Notes, Questions, Thoughts, Musings*

_____

_____

_____

_____

_____

_____

_____

_____

_____

_____

_____

_____

_____

_____

_____

_____

_____

_____

_____

_____

_____

_____

_____

_____

_____

DAY 24

Note 2 Self: *"People's negative opinions of you are just that—opinions. Don't do anything that will make them fact."*

1) *Reflect*: What do you believe this means? What does it say to you?

_____
_____
_____
_____
_____
_____
_____

2) *Relate*: How does this connect with your life/experiences? Describe a memory, experience or feeling that you've had as a result of this note.

_____
_____
_____
_____
_____
_____

3) *Release Yourself:* What actions will you release yourself to take in your life as a result of today's note?

_____
_____
_____
_____
_____
_____
_____

4) Your Own Notes, Questions, Thoughts, Musings

DAY 25

Note 2 Self: *"Taking responsibility is empowering because that means you are in control."*

1) *Reflect*: What do you believe this means? What does it say to you?

_____

_____

_____

_____

_____

_____

_____

2) *Relate*: How does this connect with your life/experiences? Describe a memory, experience or feeling that you've had as a result of this note.

_____

_____

_____

_____

_____

_____

3) *Release Yourself*: What actions will you release yourself to take in your life as a result of today's note?

_____

_____

_____

_____

_____

_____

4) *Your Own Notes, Questions, Thoughts, Musings*

_____

_____

_____

_____

_____

_____

_____

_____

_____

_____

_____

_____

_____

_____

_____

_____

_____

_____

_____

_____

_____

_____

_____

_____

_____

DAY 26

Note 2 Self: **"When you focus your energy solely on what you don't have; you diminish the greatest thing that you <u>do</u> have--yourself."**

1) *Reflect*: What do you believe this means? What does it say to you?

_____

_____

_____

_____

_____

_____

_____

2) *Relate*: How does this connect with your life/experiences? Describe a memory, experience or feeling that you've had as a result of this note.

_____

_____

_____

_____

_____

3) *Release Yourself*: What actions will you release yourself to take in your life as a result of today's note?

_____

_____

_____

_____

_____

_____

4) *Your Own Notes, Questions, Thoughts, Musings*

_____

_____

_____

_____

_____

_____

_____

_____

_____

_____

_____

_____

_____

_____

_____

_____

_____

_____

_____

_____

_____

_____

_____

_____

_____

_____

DAY 27

Note 2 Self: "What ultimately matters most is not what others think of you, or how they view you, but what you think of and how you view yourself."

1) **Reflect**: What do you believe this means? What does it say to you?

_____
_____
_____
_____
_____
_____

2) **Relate**: How does this connect with your life/experiences? Describe a memory, experience or feeling that you've had as a result of this note.

_____
_____
_____
_____
_____

3) **Release Yourself**: What actions will you release yourself to take in your life as a result of today's note?

_____
_____
_____
_____
_____
_____

4) *Your Own Notes, Questions, Thoughts, Musings*

_____

_____

_____

_____

_____

_____

_____

_____

_____

_____

_____

_____

_____

_____

_____

_____

_____

_____

_____

_____

_____

_____

_____

_____

_____

_____

DAY 28

Note 2 Self: "If you don't want to be taken advantage of—stop giving others the advantage."

1) **Reflect**: What do you believe this means? What does it say to you?

_____
_____
_____
_____
_____
_____
_____

2) **Relate**: How does this connect with your life/experiences? Describe a memory, experience or feeling that you've had as a result of this note.

_____
_____
_____
_____
_____
_____

3) **Release Yourself**: What actions will you release yourself to take in your life as a result of today's note?

_____
_____
_____
_____
_____
_____
_____

4) *Your Own Notes, Questions, Thoughts, Musings*

DAY 29

***Note 2 Self:* "It's never too late to get the life you want to have. But then again, it's never too early either."**

1) *Reflect*: What do you believe this means? What does it say to you?

_____

_____

_____

_____

_____

_____

_____

2) *Relate*: How does this connect with your life/experiences? Describe a memory, experience or feeling that you've had as a result of this note.

_____

_____

_____

_____

_____

_____

3) *Release Yourself*: What actions will you release yourself to take in your life as a result of today's note?

_____

_____

_____

_____

_____

_____

4) *Your Own Notes, Questions, Thoughts, Musings*

_____

_____

_____

_____

_____

_____

_____

_____

_____

_____

_____

_____

_____

_____

_____

_____

_____

_____

_____

_____

_____

_____

_____

_____

_____

_____

DAY 30

Note 2 Self: *"If you constantly say you're "trying" to do something; what you're really saying is that you're actually not getting it done."*

1) *Reflect*: What do you believe this means? What does it say to you?

_____

_____

_____

_____

_____

_____

_____

2) *Relate*: How does this connect with your life/experiences? Describe a memory, experience or feeling that you've had as a result of this note.

_____

_____

_____

_____

_____

_____

3) *Release Yourself*: What actions will you release yourself to take in your life as a result of today's note?

_____

_____

_____

_____

_____

_____

4) *Your Own Notes, Questions, Thoughts, Musings*

_____

_____

_____

_____

_____

_____

_____

_____

_____

_____

_____

_____

_____

_____

_____

_____

_____

_____

_____

_____

_____

_____

_____

_____

30-Day Check-in!

Through the Looking Glass

Congratulations! You have made it through the first 30 days of "Note 2 Self". Take a moment to reflect on the process that you've undertaken.

What changes do you notice in yourself?

What was hard? What was easy?

What is better? What is different?

What do you want to do and/or be from this point?

_____

_____

_____

_____

_____

_____

_____

_____

_____

_____

_____

_____

_____

KEISHA A. RIVERS-SHORTY

Part 2 Begins!

DAY 31

Note 2 Self: "There is no greater prison than your own limited thinking."

1) *Reflect*: What do you believe this means? What does it say to you?

_____

_____

_____

_____

_____

_____

_____

2) *Relate*: How does this connect with your life/experiences? Describe a memory, experience or feeling that you've had as a result of this note.

_____

_____

_____

_____

_____

_____

3) *Release Yourself:* What actions will you release yourself to take in your life as a result of today's note?

_____

_____

_____

_____

_____

_____

_____

4) *Your Own Notes, Questions, Thoughts, Musings*

_____

_____

_____

_____

_____

_____

_____

_____

_____

_____

_____

_____

_____

_____

_____

_____

_____

_____

_____

_____

_____

_____

_____

_____

_____

_____

DAY 32

Note 2 Self: "Sometimes you have to make the decision to close a door so another can open."

1) *Reflect*: What do you believe this means? What does it say to you?

_____
_____
_____
_____
_____
_____
_____

2) *Relate*: How does this connect with your life/experiences? Describe a memory, experience or feeling that you've had as a result of this note.

_____
_____
_____
_____
_____
_____

3) *Release Yourself:* What actions will you release yourself to take in your life as a result of today's note?

_____
_____
_____
_____
_____
_____
_____
_____

4) *Your Own Notes, Questions, Thoughts, Musings*

_____

_____

_____

_____

_____

_____

_____

_____

_____

_____

_____

_____

_____

_____

_____

_____

_____

_____

_____

_____

_____

_____

_____

_____

_____

_____

_____

DAY 33

Note 2 Self: "Just for today—be your own destiny."

1) **Reflect**: What do you believe this means? What does it say to you?

_____
_____
_____
_____
_____
_____
_____

2) **Relate**: How does this connect with your life/experiences? Describe a memory, experience or feeling that you've had as a result of this note.

_____
_____
_____
_____
_____
_____

3) **Release Yourself**: What actions will you release yourself to take in your life as a result of today's note?

_____
_____
_____
_____
_____
_____
_____
_____

4) *Your Own Notes, Questions, Thoughts, Musings*

_____

_____

_____

_____

_____

_____

_____

_____

_____

_____

_____

_____

_____

_____

_____

_____

_____

_____

_____

_____

_____

_____

_____

_____

_____

DAY 34

Note 2 Self: "Sometimes the vision you have for your life is smaller than the vision life has for you."

1) **Reflect**: What do you believe this means? What does it say to you?

_____

_____

_____

_____

_____

_____

_____

2) **Relate**: How does this connect with your life/experiences? Describe a memory, experience or feeling that you've had as a result of this note.

_____

_____

_____

_____

_____

3) **Release Yourself**: What actions will you release yourself to take in your life as a result of today's note?

_____

_____

_____

_____

_____

_____

_____

4) *Your Own Notes, Questions, Thoughts, Musings*

_____

_____

_____

_____

_____

_____

_____

_____

_____

_____

_____

_____

_____

_____

_____

_____

_____

_____

_____

_____

_____

_____

_____

_____

_____

_____

_____

DAY 35

Note 2 Self: "Sometimes it's okay to revisit things, people, places and memories from your past. Just make sure not to make it an extended stay. You moved on for a reason."

1) **Reflect**: What do you believe this means? What does it say to you?

   _____
   _____
   _____
   _____
   _____
   _____

2) **Relate**: How does this connect with your life/experiences? Describe a memory, experience or feeling that you've had as a result of this note.

   _____
   _____
   _____
   _____
   _____

3) **Release Yourself**: What actions will you release yourself to take in your life as a result of today's note?

   _____
   _____
   _____
   _____
   _____
   _____
   _____

4) *Your Own Notes, Questions, Thoughts, Musings*

_____
_____
_____
_____
_____
_____
_____
_____
_____
_____
_____
_____
_____
_____
_____
_____
_____
_____
_____
_____
_____
_____
_____
_____
_____
_____

DAY 36

Note 2 Self: "Being 'alive' is more than a state of being. It is an act of living."

1) *Reflect*: What do you believe this means? What does it say to you?

_____

_____

_____

_____

_____

_____

_____

2) *Relate*: How does this connect with your life/experiences? Describe a memory, experience or feeling that you've had as a result of this note.

_____

_____

_____

_____

_____

_____

3) *Release Yourself*: What actions will you release yourself to take in your life as a result of today's note?

_____

_____

_____

_____

_____

_____

_____

_____

4) **Your Own Notes, Questions, Thoughts, Musings**

_____

_____

_____

_____

_____

_____

_____

_____

_____

_____

_____

_____

_____

_____

_____

_____

_____

_____

_____

_____

_____

_____

_____

_____

_____

_____

_____

DAY 37

Note 2 Self: **"In the grand scheme of things, little things are just that—little things. Don't make them bigger than they need to be."**

1) *Reflect*: What do you believe this means? What does it say to you?

_____

_____

_____

_____

_____

_____

_____

2) *Relate*: How does this connect with your life/experiences? Describe a memory, experience or feeling that you've had as a result of this note.

_____

_____

_____

_____

_____

3) *Release Yourself*: What actions will you release yourself to take in your life as a result of today's note?

_____

_____

_____

_____

_____

_____

_____

4) Your Own Notes, Questions, Thoughts, Musings

_____

_____

_____

_____

_____

_____

_____

_____

_____

_____

_____

_____

_____

_____

_____

_____

_____

_____

_____

_____

_____

_____

_____

_____

DAY 38

Note 2 Self: "You never know how strong you truly are until you have to endure."

1) **Reflect**: What do you believe this means? What does it say to you?

_____
_____
_____
_____
_____
_____
_____

2) **Relate**: How does this connect with your life/experiences? Describe a memory, experience or feeling that you've had as a result of this note.

_____
_____
_____
_____
_____
_____

3) **Release Yourself**: What actions will you release yourself to take in your life as a result of today's note?

_____
_____
_____
_____
_____
_____
_____
_____

4) *Your Own Notes, Questions, Thoughts, Musings*

_____

_____

_____

_____

_____

_____

_____

_____

_____

_____

_____

_____

_____

_____

_____

_____

_____

_____

_____

_____

_____

_____

_____

_____

_____

DAY 39

Note 2 Self: **"The change you seek in life begins with you."**

1) **Reflect**: What do you believe this means? What does it say to you?

_____
_____
_____
_____
_____
_____
_____

2) **Relate**: How does this connect with your life/experiences? Describe a memory, experience or feeling that you've had as a result of this note.

_____
_____
_____
_____
_____
_____

3) **Release Yourself:** What actions will you release yourself to take in your life as a result of today's note?

_____
_____
_____
_____
_____
_____
_____

4) *Your Own Notes, Questions, Thoughts, Musings*

_____

_____

_____

_____

_____

_____

_____

_____

_____

_____

_____

_____

_____

_____

_____

_____

_____

_____

_____

_____

_____

_____

_____

_____

_____

_____

_____

_____

DAY 40

Note 2 Self: "What's amazing is that the one thing that holds most people back from achieving their true potential is the thing they create in their own minds—FEAR."

1) *Reflect*: What do you believe this means? What does it say to you?

_____

_____

_____

_____

_____

_____

2) *Relate*: How does this connect with your life/experiences? Describe a memory, experience or feeling that you've had as a result of this note.

_____

_____

_____

_____

_____

3) *Release Yourself*: What actions will you release yourself to take in your life as a result of today's note?

_____

_____

_____

_____

_____

_____

_____

4) Your Own Notes, Questions, Thoughts, Musings

_____

_____

_____

_____

_____

_____

_____

_____

_____

_____

_____

_____

_____

_____

_____

_____

_____

_____

_____

_____

_____

_____

_____

_____

DAY 41

Note 2 Self: "Those things that we spend a lifetime searching for can usually be found once we turn our focus inward, not outward."

1) *Reflect*: What do you believe this means? What does it say to you?

_____

_____

_____

_____

_____

_____

_____

2) *Relate*: How does this connect with your life/experiences? Describe a memory, experience or feeling that you've had as a result of this note.

_____

_____

_____

_____

_____

_____

3) *Release Yourself*: What actions will you release yourself to take in your life as a result of today's note?

_____

_____

_____

_____

_____

_____

4) *Your Own Notes, Questions, Thoughts, Musings*

_____

_____

_____

_____

_____

_____

_____

_____

_____

_____

_____

_____

_____

_____

_____

_____

_____

_____

_____

_____

_____

_____

_____

_____

_____

DAY 42

Note 2 Self: "Don't agonize too much over "things" you have lost. What is of most value are the things you carry within your heart, remember in your mind and feel in your soul."

1) *Reflect*: What do you believe this means? What does it say to you?

_____

_____

_____

_____

_____

_____

2) *Relate*: How does this connect with your life/experiences? Describe a memory, experience or feeling that you've had as a result of this note.

_____

_____

_____

_____

_____

3) *Release Yourself:* What actions will you release yourself to take in your life as a result of today's note?

_____

_____

_____

_____

_____

_____

4) *Your Own Notes, Questions, Thoughts, Musings*

_____

_____

_____

_____

_____

_____

_____

_____

_____

_____

_____

_____

_____

_____

_____

_____

_____

_____

_____

_____

_____

_____

_____

_____

DAY 43

Note 2 Self: "Every day is a new journey; every experience a new memory—make yours a good one."

1) **Reflect**: What do you believe this means? What does it say to you?

_____

_____

_____

_____

_____

_____

_____

2) **Relate**: How does this connect with your life/experiences? Describe a memory, experience or feeling that you've had as a result of this note.

_____

_____

_____

_____

_____

_____

3) **Release Yourself:** What actions will you release yourself to take in your life as a result of today's note?

_____

_____

_____

_____

_____

_____

4) *Your Own Notes, Questions, Thoughts, Musings*

_____

_____

_____

_____

_____

_____

_____

_____

_____

_____

_____

_____

_____

_____

_____

_____

_____

_____

_____

_____

_____

_____

_____

_____

_____

DAY 44

Note 2 Self: "Find the right balance of push and pull; stop and go; motivation and caution that keeps you sane, happy and moving ahead."

1) *Reflect*: What do you believe this means? What does it say to you?

_____

_____

_____

_____

_____

_____

_____

2) *Relate*: How does this connect with your life/experiences? Describe a memory, experience or feeling that you've had as a result of this note.

_____

_____

_____

_____

_____

3) *Release Yourself*: What actions will you release yourself to take in your life as a result of today's note?

_____

_____

_____

_____

_____

_____

_____

_____

4) *Your Own Notes, Questions, Thoughts, Musings*

_____

_____

_____

_____

_____

_____

_____

_____

_____

_____

_____

_____

_____

_____

_____

_____

_____

_____

_____

_____

_____

_____

_____

_____

_____

DAY 45

Note 2 Self: "Change and progress come from reflection and practice. You can't move forward if you don't understand where you are, where you've been or where you want to go."

1) **Reflect**: What do you believe this means? What does it say to you?

_____

_____

_____

_____

_____

_____

2) **Relate**: How does this connect with your life/experiences? Describe a memory, experience or feeling that you've had as a result of this note.

_____

_____

_____

_____

_____

3) **Release Yourself**: What actions will you release yourself to take in your life as a result of today's note?

_____

_____

_____

_____

_____

_____

_____

4) *Your Own Notes, Questions, Thoughts, Musings*

_____

_____

_____

_____

_____

_____

_____

_____

_____

_____

_____

_____

_____

_____

_____

_____

_____

_____

_____

_____

_____

_____

_____

_____

_____

_____

DAY 46

Note 2 Self: *"We must truly understand and embrace who we are so that we may become that which we are meant to be."*

1) **Reflect**: What do you believe this means? What does it say to you?

_____
_____
_____
_____
_____
_____
_____

2) **Relate**: How does this connect with your life/experiences? Describe a memory, experience or feeling that you've had as a result of this note.

_____
_____
_____
_____
_____
_____

3) **Release Yourself**: What actions will you release yourself to take in your life as a result of today's note?

_____
_____
_____
_____
_____
_____
_____

4) *Your Own Notes, Questions, Thoughts, Musings*

_____

_____

_____

_____

_____

_____

_____

_____

_____

_____

_____

_____

_____

_____

_____

_____

_____

_____

_____

_____

_____

_____

_____

_____

_____

_____

_____

DAY 47

Note 2 Self: "To want to be someone else is an insult to you."

1) **Reflect**: What do you believe this means? What does it say to you?

_____
_____
_____
_____
_____
_____
_____

2) **Relate**: How does this connect with your life/experiences? Describe a memory, experience or feeling that you've had as a result of this note.

_____
_____
_____
_____
_____
_____

3) **Release Yourself**: What actions will you release yourself to take in your life as a result of today's note?

_____
_____
_____
_____
_____
_____
_____
_____

4) *Your Own Notes, Questions, Thoughts, Musings*

_____

_____

_____

_____

_____

_____

_____

_____

_____

_____

_____

_____

_____

_____

_____

_____

_____

_____

_____

_____

_____

_____

_____

_____

_____

_____

_____

DAY 48

Note 2 Self: "Stop trying to convince people of how great/valuable you are and just do and be the best you can. Recognition will come with action and results."

1) **Reflect**: What do you believe this means? What does it say to you?

_____

_____

_____

_____

_____

_____

2) **Relate**: How does this connect with your life/experiences? Describe a memory, experience or feeling that you've had as a result of this note.

_____

_____

_____

_____

_____

3) **Release Yourself**: What actions will you release yourself to take in your life as a result of today's note?

_____

_____

_____

_____

_____

_____

_____

_____

4) *Your Own Notes, Questions, Thoughts, Musings*

_____

_____

_____

_____

_____

_____

_____

_____

_____

_____

_____

_____

_____

_____

_____

_____

_____

_____

_____

_____

_____

_____

_____

_____

_____

DAY 49

Note 2 Self: "The person you are and the person you hope to become are not that far apart. Take the necessary steps to make them one."

1) **Reflect**: What do you believe this means? What does it say to you?

_____

_____

_____

_____

_____

_____

_____

2) **Relate**: How does this connect with your life/experiences? Describe a memory, experience or feeling that you've had as a result of this note.

_____

_____

_____

_____

_____

_____

3) **Release Yourself**: What actions will you release yourself to take in your life as a result of today's note?

_____

_____

_____

_____

_____

_____

_____

4)   *Your Own Notes, Questions, Thoughts, Musings*

_____

_____

_____

_____

_____

_____

_____

_____

_____

_____

_____

_____

_____

_____

_____

_____

_____

_____

_____

_____

_____

_____

_____

_____

_____

_____

DAY 50

Note 2 Self: "It's not always about getting to the 'big goals' all at once. Smaller goals achieved over time are just as important and will ultimately get you to your final destination."

1) **Reflect**: What do you believe this means? What does it say to you?

   _____
   _____
   _____
   _____
   _____
   _____

2) **Relate**: How does this connect with your life/experiences? Describe a memory, experience or feeling that you've had as a result of this note.

   _____
   _____
   _____
   _____
   _____

3) **Release Yourself:** What actions will you release yourself to take in your life as a result of today's note?

   _____
   _____
   _____
   _____
   _____
   _____
   _____
   _____

4) *Your Own Notes, Questions, Thoughts, Musings*

_____

_____

_____

_____

_____

_____

_____

_____

_____

_____

_____

_____

_____

_____

_____

_____

_____

_____

_____

_____

_____

_____

_____

_____

_____

_____

_____

DAY 51

Note 2 Self: "Your journey is not without detours, stops, starts, mountains, hills and valleys, but what truly defines you is not your ultimate destination, but the spirit in which you approach every turn and change in direction along the way."

1) **Reflect**: What do you believe this means? What does it say to you?

   _____

   _____

   _____

   _____

   _____

2) **Relate**: How does this connect with your life/experiences? Describe a memory, experience or feeling that you've had as a result of this note.

   _____

   _____

   _____

   _____

3) **Release Yourself**: What actions will you release yourself to take in your life as a result of today's note?

   _____

   _____

   _____

   _____

   _____

   _____

   _____

   _____

4) *Your Own Notes, Questions, Thoughts, Musings*

_____

_____

_____

_____

_____

_____

_____

_____

_____

_____

_____

_____

_____

_____

_____

_____

_____

_____

_____

_____

_____

_____

_____

_____

_____

DAY 52

Note 2 Self: "The distance between how your life is and how you want your life to be is measured in how far your determination stretches."

1) **Reflect**: What do you believe this means? What does it say to you?

_____

_____

_____

_____

_____

_____

2) **Relate**: How does this connect with your life/experiences? Describe a memory, experience or feeling that you've had as a result of this note.

_____

_____

_____

_____

_____

_____

3) **Release Yourself**: What actions will you release yourself to take in your life as a result of today's note?

_____

_____

_____

_____

_____

_____

_____

4) *Your Own Notes, Questions, Thoughts, Musings*

_____

_____

_____

_____

_____

_____

_____

_____

_____

_____

_____

_____

_____

_____

_____

_____

_____

_____

_____

_____

_____

_____

_____

_____

_____

DAY 53

Note 2 Self: "Instead of asking 'why me?', try asking 'why NOT me?--and get out there and do it!"

1) **Reflect**: What do you believe this means? What does it say to you?

_____
_____
_____
_____
_____
_____

2) **Relate**: How does this connect with your life/experiences? Describe a memory, experience or feeling that you've had as a result of this note.

_____
_____
_____
_____
_____
_____

3) **Release Yourself**: What actions will you release yourself to take in your life as a result of today's note?

_____
_____
_____
_____
_____
_____
_____
_____

4) *Your Own Notes, Questions, Thoughts, Musings*

_____

_____

_____

_____

_____

_____

_____

_____

_____

_____

_____

_____

_____

_____

_____

_____

_____

_____

_____

_____

_____

_____

_____

_____

_____

_____

DAY 54

Note 2 Self: "Stop living your life 'in theory'.
Most times the thing you are most afraid of doing
is the most worthwhile."

1) *Reflect*: What do you believe this means? What does it say to you?

_____
_____
_____
_____
_____
_____
_____

2) *Relate*: How does this connect with your life/experiences? Describe a memory, experience or feeling that you've had as a result of this note.

_____
_____
_____
_____
_____
_____

3) *Release Yourself*: What actions will you release yourself to take in your life as a result of today's note?

_____
_____
_____
_____
_____
_____
_____

4) Your Own Notes, Questions, Thoughts, Musings

_____

_____

_____

_____

_____

_____

_____

_____

_____

_____

_____

_____

_____

_____

_____

_____

_____

_____

_____

_____

_____

_____

_____

_____

_____

_____

DAY 55

Note 2 Self: "Life already 'is'. You have to decide and take action on what you want life to 'be'."

1) **Reflect**: What do you believe this means? What does it say to you?

_____

_____

_____

_____

_____

_____

_____

2) **Relate**: How does this connect with your life/experiences? Describe a memory, experience or feeling that you've had as a result of this note.

_____

_____

_____

_____

_____

_____

3) **Release Yourself**: What actions will you release yourself to take in your life as a result of today's note?

_____

_____

_____

_____

_____

_____

_____

4) *Your Own Notes, Questions, Thoughts, Musings*

_____

_____

_____

_____

_____

_____

_____

_____

_____

_____

_____

_____

_____

_____

_____

_____

_____

_____

_____

_____

_____

_____

_____

_____

_____

_____

DAY 56

Note 2 Self: "It's not always about what you get out of it, but rather what you put into it."

1) **Reflect**: What do you believe this means? What does it say to you?

_____

_____

_____

_____

_____

_____

_____

2) **Relate**: How does this connect with your life/experiences? Describe a memory, experience or feeling that you've had as a result of this note.

_____

_____

_____

_____

_____

_____

3) **Release Yourself**: What actions will you release yourself to take in your life as a result of today's note?

_____

_____

_____

_____

_____

_____

_____

4) *Your Own Notes, Questions, Thoughts, Musings*

_____

_____

_____

_____

_____

_____

_____

_____

_____

_____

_____

_____

_____

_____

_____

_____

_____

_____

_____

_____

_____

_____

_____

_____

_____

DAY 57

Note 2 Self: "The life you live is yours to create."

1) **Reflect**: What do you believe this means? What does it say to you?

_____

_____

_____

_____

_____

_____

_____

2) **Relate**: How does this connect with your life/experiences? Describe a memory, experience or feeling that you've had as a result of this note.

_____

_____

_____

_____

_____

_____

3) **Release Yourself:** What actions will you release yourself to take in your life as a result of today's note?

_____

_____

_____

_____

_____

_____

_____

4) ***Your Own Notes, Questions, Thoughts, Musings***

_____

_____

_____

_____

_____

_____

_____

_____

_____

_____

_____

_____

_____

_____

_____

_____

_____

_____

_____

_____

_____

_____

_____

_____

_____

DAY 58

Note 2 Self: *"Sometimes you have to back up to go forward."*

1) **Reflect**: What do you believe this means? What does it say to you?

_____
_____
_____
_____
_____
_____
_____

2) **Relate**: How does this connect with your life/experiences? Describe a memory, experience or feeling that you've had as a result of this note.

_____
_____
_____
_____
_____
_____

3) **Release Yourself**: What actions will you release yourself to take in your life as a result of today's note?

_____
_____
_____
_____
_____
_____
_____
_____

4) *Your Own Notes, Questions, Thoughts, Musings*

_____

_____

_____

_____

_____

_____

_____

_____

_____

_____

_____

_____

_____

_____

_____

_____

_____

_____

_____

_____

_____

_____

_____

_____

_____

DAY 59

Note 2 Self: "Fearing the best is a complete waste of time."

1) **Reflect**: What do you believe this means? What does it say to you?

_____

_____

_____

_____

_____

_____

_____

2) **Relate**: How does this connect with your life/experiences? Describe a memory, experience or feeling that you've had as a result of this note.

_____

_____

_____

_____

_____

_____

3) **Release Yourself:** What actions will you release yourself to take in your life as a result of today's note?

_____

_____

_____

_____

_____

_____

_____

4) *Your Own Notes, Questions, Thoughts, Musings*

_____

_____

_____

_____

_____

_____

_____

_____

_____

_____

_____

_____

_____

_____

_____

_____

_____

_____

_____

_____

_____

_____

_____

_____

DAY 60

Note 2 Self: "Don't let your fear of the greatness that is within you stop you from being your greatest you."

1) **Reflect**: What do you believe this means? What does it say to you?

_____
_____
_____
_____
_____
_____
_____

2) **Relate**: How does this connect with your life/experiences? Describe a memory, experience or feeling that you've had as a result of this note.

_____
_____
_____
_____
_____
_____

3) **Release Yourself**: What actions will you release yourself to take in your life as a result of today's note?

_____
_____
_____
_____
_____
_____
_____

4) *Your Own Notes, Questions, Thoughts, Musings*

_____

_____

_____

_____

_____

_____

_____

_____

_____

_____

_____

_____

_____

_____

_____

_____

_____

_____

_____

_____

_____

_____

_____

_____

60-Day Check-in!

Through the Looking Glass

Congratulations! You have made it through the first 60 days of "Note 2 Self". Take a moment to reflect on the process that you've undertaken.

What changes do you notice in yourself?

What was hard? What was easy?

What is better? What is different?

What do you want to do and/or be from this point?

_____

_____

_____

_____

_____

_____

_____

_____

_____

_____

_____

_____

_____

Part 3 Begins!

DAY 61

Note 2 Self: "Just for this moment—be the person you know you can be. Now repeat."

1) **Reflect**: What do you believe this means? What does it say to you?

_____

_____

_____

_____

_____

_____

_____

2) **Relate**: How does this connect with your life/experiences? Describe a memory, experience or feeling that you've had as a result of this note.

_____

_____

_____

_____

_____

_____

3) **Release Yourself**: What actions will you release yourself to take in your life as a result of today's note?

_____

_____

_____

_____

_____

_____

_____

4) *Your Own Notes, Questions, Thoughts, Musings*

_____

_____

_____

_____

_____

_____

_____

_____

_____

_____

_____

_____

_____

_____

_____

_____

_____

_____

_____

_____

_____

_____

_____

_____

_____

_____

DAY 62

Note 2 Self: *"The starting point to creating a new path for yourself is usually at the intersection of fear and frustration."*

1) *Reflect*: What do you believe this means? What does it say to you?

_____

_____

_____

_____

_____

_____

_____

2) *Relate*: How does this connect with your life/experiences? Describe a memory, experience or feeling that you've had as a result of this note.

_____

_____

_____

_____

_____

_____

3) *Release Yourself*: What actions will you release yourself to take in your life as a result of today's note?

_____

_____

_____

_____

_____

_____

_____

4) *Your Own Notes, Questions, Thoughts, Musings*

_____

_____

_____

_____

_____

_____

_____

_____

_____

_____

_____

_____

_____

_____

_____

_____

_____

_____

_____

_____

_____

_____

_____

_____

_____

DAY 63

Note 2 Self: *"In the grand scheme of things, you may be only one person; but to one person you are grand in the scheme of things."*

1) **Reflect**: What do you believe this means? What does it say to you?

_____

_____

_____

_____

_____

_____

_____

2) **Relate**: How does this connect with your life/experiences? Describe a memory, experience or feeling that you've had as a result of this note.

_____

_____

_____

_____

_____

_____

3) **Release Yourself**: What actions will you release yourself to take in your life as a result of today's note?

_____

_____

_____

_____

_____

_____

_____

4) Your Own Notes, Questions, Thoughts, Musings

_____

_____

_____

_____

_____

_____

_____

_____

_____

_____

_____

_____

_____

_____

_____

_____

_____

_____

_____

_____

_____

_____

_____

_____

_____

_____

_____

_____

DAY 64

Note 2 Self: "In all the flurry of activity that is your day to day life—don't forget to take a few moments to close your eyes and take a few deep, cleaning breaths to center you, help you focus and keep you on track."

1) **Reflect**: What do you believe this means? What does it say to you?

_____
_____
_____
_____
_____
_____

2) **Relate**: How does this connect with your life/experiences? Describe a memory, experience or feeling that you've had as a result of this note.

_____
_____
_____
_____
_____

3) **Release Yourself**: What actions will you release yourself to take in your life as a result of today's note?

_____
_____
_____
_____
_____
_____
_____

4) Your Own Notes, Questions, Thoughts, Musings

_____

_____

_____

_____

_____

_____

_____

_____

_____

_____

_____

_____

_____

_____

_____

_____

_____

_____

_____

_____

_____

_____

_____

_____

_____

_____

_____

DAY 65

Note 2 Self: "There is greatness within you already. Share it with your little slice of the world and the rest will take care of itself."

1) **Reflect**: What do you believe this means? What does it say to you?

_____

_____

_____

_____

_____

_____

2) **Relate**: How does this connect with your life/experiences? Describe a memory, experience or feeling that you've had as a result of this note.

_____

_____

_____

_____

_____

3) **Release Yourself**: What actions will you release yourself to take in your life as a result of today's note?

_____

_____

_____

_____

_____

_____

4) *Your Own Notes, Questions, Thoughts, Musings*

_____

_____

_____

_____

_____

_____

_____

_____

_____

_____

_____

_____

_____

_____

_____

_____

_____

_____

_____

_____

_____

_____

_____

_____

_____

_____

DAY 66

Note 2 Self: "Only when you are honest with yourself can you truly be honest with others."

1) *Reflect*: What do you believe this means? What does it say to you?

_____

_____

_____

_____

_____

_____

2) *Relate*: How does this connect with your life/experiences? Describe a memory, experience or feeling that you've had as a result of this note.

_____

_____

_____

_____

_____

3) *Release Yourself:* What actions will you release yourself to take in your life as a result of today's note?

_____

_____

_____

_____

_____

_____

_____

4) *Your Own Notes, Questions, Thoughts, Musings*

_____

_____

_____

_____

_____

_____

_____

_____

_____

_____

_____

_____

_____

_____

_____

_____

_____

_____

_____

_____

_____

_____

_____

_____

DAY 67

Note 2 Self: *"When you look back at the trials, setbacks and troubles of your past, realize that you're standing today—so that means you're a lot stronger that you thought."*

1) *Reflect*: What do you believe this means? What does it say to you?

_____

_____

_____

_____

_____

_____

2) *Relate*: How does this connect with your life/experiences? Describe a memory, experience or feeling that you've had as a result of this note.

_____

_____

_____

_____

_____

3) *Release Yourself*: What actions will you release yourself to take in your life as a result of today's note?

_____

_____

_____

_____

_____

_____

_____

4) *Your Own Notes, Questions, Thoughts, Musings*

_____

_____

_____

_____

_____

_____

_____

_____

_____

_____

_____

_____

_____

_____

_____

_____

_____

_____

_____

_____

_____

_____

_____

_____

_____

_____

DAY 68

Note 2 Self: "For everything in your life there is a reason and a season. When there is no longer a reason, the season has ended, so just let it go."

1) **Reflect**: What do you believe this means? What does it say to you?

_____

_____

_____

_____

_____

_____

_____

2) **Relate**: How does this connect with your life/experiences? Describe a memory, experience or feeling that you've had as a result of this note.

_____

_____

_____

_____

_____

_____

3) **Release Yourself**: What actions will you release yourself to take in your life as a result of today's note?

_____

_____

_____

_____

_____

_____

_____

4) *Your Own Notes, Questions, Thoughts, Musings*

_____

_____

_____

_____

_____

_____

_____

_____

_____

_____

_____

_____

_____

_____

_____

_____

_____

_____

_____

_____

_____

_____

_____

_____

_____

DAY 69

Note 2 Self: *"The life you live is the life you choose for yourself."*

1) **Reflect**: What do you believe this means? What does it say to you?

_____

_____

_____

_____

_____

_____

_____

2) **Relate**: How does this connect with your life/experiences? Describe a memory, experience or feeling that you've had as a result of this note.

_____

_____

_____

_____

_____

_____

3) **Release Yourself**: What actions will you release yourself to take in your life as a result of today's note?

_____

_____

_____

_____

_____

_____

_____

4) Your Own Notes, Questions, Thoughts, Musings

DAY 70

Note 2 Self: "In your life, decide what you truly need and then figure out how to ask for it."

1) **Reflect**: What do you believe this means? What does it say to you?

_____
_____
_____
_____
_____
_____
_____

2) **Relate**: How does this connect with your life/experiences? Describe a memory, experience or feeling that you've had as a result of this note.

_____
_____
_____
_____
_____
_____

3) **Release Yourself**: What actions will you release yourself to take in your life as a result of today's note?

_____
_____
_____
_____
_____
_____
_____
_____

4) *Your Own Notes, Questions, Thoughts, Musings*

_____

_____

_____

_____

_____

_____

_____

_____

_____

_____

_____

_____

_____

_____

_____

_____

_____

_____

_____

_____

_____

_____

_____

_____

_____

_____

DAY 71

Note 2 Self: "Give yourself permission—to dream, to hope, to laugh, to cry, to succeed, to fail, to love, to lose—to LIVE."

1) **Reflect**: What do you believe this means? What does it say to you?

_____

_____

_____

_____

_____

_____

_____

2) **Relate**: How does this connect with your life/experiences? Describe a memory, experience or feeling that you've had as a result of this note.

_____

_____

_____

_____

_____

_____

3) **Release Yourself**: What actions will you release yourself to take in your life as a result of today's note?

_____

_____

_____

_____

_____

_____

_____

4) Your Own Notes, Questions, Thoughts, Musings

_____

_____

_____

_____

_____

_____

_____

_____

_____

_____

_____

_____

_____

_____

_____

_____

_____

_____

_____

_____

_____

_____

_____

_____

_____

DAY 72

Note 2 Self: "It doesn't matter at what speed you're moving, as long as you keep going."

1) **Reflect**: What do you believe this means? What does it say to you?

_____
_____
_____
_____
_____
_____
_____

2) **Relate**: How does this connect with your life/experiences? Describe a memory, experience or feeling that you've had as a result of this note.

_____
_____
_____
_____
_____
_____

3) **Release Yourself**: What actions will you release yourself to take in your life as a result of today's note?

_____
_____
_____
_____
_____
_____
_____

4) *Your Own Notes, Questions, Thoughts, Musings*

DAY 73

Note 2 Self: "*You are uniquely qualified to be YOU—so embrace yourself in all your imperfect glory. Take everything about you in stride and use it to create the life that you want to have.*"

1) *Reflect*: What do you believe this means? What does it say to you?

_____
_____
_____
_____
_____
_____

2) *Relate*: How does this connect with your life/experiences? Describe a memory, experience or feeling that you've had as a result of this note.

_____
_____
_____
_____

3) *Release Yourself:* What actions will you release yourself to take in your life as a result of today's note?

_____
_____
_____
_____
_____
_____
_____

4) *Your Own Notes, Questions, Thoughts, Musings*

_____

_____

_____

_____

_____

_____

_____

_____

_____

_____

_____

_____

_____

_____

_____

_____

_____

_____

_____

_____

_____

_____

_____

_____

DAY 74

Note 2 Self: "*We are attracted to those who are most like who we want to be.*"

1) *Reflect*: What do you believe this means? What does it say to you?

_____

_____

_____

_____

_____

_____

_____

2) *Relate*: How does this connect with your life/experiences? Describe a memory, experience or feeling that you've had as a result of this note.

_____

_____

_____

_____

_____

_____

3) *Release Yourself:* What actions will you release yourself to take in your life as a result of today's note?

_____

_____

_____

_____

_____

_____

_____

4) *Your Own Notes, Questions, Thoughts, Musings*

_____

_____

_____

_____

_____

_____

_____

_____

_____

_____

_____

_____

_____

_____

_____

_____

_____

_____

_____

_____

_____

_____

_____

_____

_____

_____

DAY 75

Note 2 Self: "*Yesterday is gone. Don't dwell on it. You have a new opportunity to make this day—this moment—all you hoped it would be. Seize your opportunity.*"

1) *Reflect*: What do you believe this means? What does it say to you?

_____

_____

_____

_____

_____

_____

2) *Relate*: How does this connect with your life/experiences? Describe a memory, experience or feeling that you've had as a result of this note.

_____

_____

_____

_____

_____

3) *Release Yourself*: What actions will you release yourself to take in your life as a result of today's note?

_____

_____

_____

_____

_____

_____

_____

4) *Your Own Notes, Questions, Thoughts, Musings*

_____

_____

_____

_____

_____

_____

_____

_____

_____

_____

_____

_____

_____

_____

_____

_____

_____

_____

_____

_____

_____

_____

_____

_____

DAY 76

Note 2 Self: "Often there is more to situations and people than meets the eye. Take the time to look deeper and consider longer before making judgments or decisions."

1) **Reflect**: What do you believe this means? What does it say to you?

_____
_____
_____
_____
_____
_____

2) **Relate**: How does this connect with your life/experiences? Describe a memory, experience or feeling that you've had as a result of this note.

_____
_____
_____
_____
_____

3) **Release Yourself**: What actions will you release yourself to take in your life as a result of today's note?

_____
_____
_____
_____
_____
_____
_____
_____

4) *Your Own Notes, Questions, Thoughts, Musings*

_____

_____

_____

_____

_____

_____

_____

_____

_____

_____

_____

_____

_____

_____

_____

_____

_____

_____

_____

_____

_____

_____

_____

_____

_____

_____

_____

DAY 77

Note 2 Self: *"You can't always control what happens to you, but you can always control how you respond to it."*

1) **Reflect:** What do you believe this means? What does it say to you?

_____

_____

_____

_____

_____

_____

_____

2) **Relate:** How does this connect with your life/experiences? Describe a memory, experience or feeling that you've had as a result of this note.

_____

_____

_____

_____

_____

3) **Release Yourself:** What actions will you release yourself to take in your life as a result of today's note?

_____

_____

_____

_____

_____

_____

_____

_____

4) *Your Own Notes, Questions, Thoughts, Musings*

_____

_____

_____

_____

_____

_____

_____

_____

_____

_____

_____

_____

_____

_____

_____

_____

_____

_____

_____

_____

_____

_____

_____

_____

_____

_____

DAY 78

Note 2 Self: "Embrace the change in your life. That's when the journey becomes interesting."

1) **Reflect**: What do you believe this means? What does it say to you?

_____

_____

_____

_____

_____

_____

_____

2) **Relate**: How does this connect with your life/experiences? Describe a memory, experience or feeling that you've had as a result of this note.

_____

_____

_____

_____

_____

_____

3) **Release Yourself**: What actions will you release yourself to take in your life as a result of today's note?

_____

_____

_____

_____

_____

_____

_____

4) Your Own Notes, Questions, Thoughts, Musings

_____

_____

_____

_____

_____

_____

_____

_____

_____

_____

_____

_____

_____

_____

_____

_____

_____

_____

_____

_____

_____

_____

_____

_____

_____

_____

DAY 79

Note 2 Self: "Forward is a general direction, not a linear progression. Sometimes you have to take a sidestep or back step in order to forward step."

1) *Reflect*: What do you believe this means? What does it say to you?

_____
_____
_____
_____
_____
_____

2) *Relate*: How does this connect with your life/experiences? Describe a memory, experience or feeling that you've had as a result of this note.

_____
_____
_____
_____
_____
_____

3) *Release Yourself*: What actions will you release yourself to take in your life as a result of today's note?

_____
_____
_____
_____
_____
_____
_____

4) Your Own Notes, Questions, Thoughts, Musings

_____

_____

_____

_____

_____

_____

_____

_____

_____

_____

_____

_____

_____

_____

_____

_____

_____

_____

_____

_____

_____

_____

_____

_____

_____

_____

DAY 80

Note 2 Self: "It is more important to know what questions to ask than to have all the answers."

1) *Reflect*: What do you believe this means? What does it say to you?

_____

_____

_____

_____

_____

_____

2) *Relate*: How does this connect with your life/experiences? Describe a memory, experience or feeling that you've had as a result of this note.

_____

_____

_____

_____

_____

_____

3) *Release Yourself*: What actions will you release yourself to take in your life as a result of today's note?

_____

_____

_____

_____

_____

_____

_____

_____

_____

4) Your Own Notes, Questions, Thoughts, Musings

DAY 81

Note 2 Self: "In all things ask yourself, 'What's the worst that could happen?'—then face it, prepare for it and overcome it."

1) **Reflect**: What do you believe this means? What does it say to you?

_____
_____
_____
_____
_____
_____
_____

2) **Relate**: How does this connect with your life/experiences? Describe a memory, experience or feeling that you've had as a result of this note.

_____
_____
_____
_____
_____
_____

3) **Release Yourself**: What actions will you release yourself to take in your life as a result of today's note?

_____
_____
_____
_____
_____
_____
_____

4) *Your Own Notes, Questions, Thoughts, Musings*

_____

_____

_____

_____

_____

_____

_____

_____

_____

_____

_____

_____

_____

_____

_____

_____

_____

_____

_____

_____

_____

_____

_____

_____

_____

_____

_____

DAY 82

Note 2 Self: *"It's not about where you've been.*
It's about where you're going."

1) ***Reflect***: What do you believe this means? What does it say to you?

_____

_____

_____

_____

_____

_____

_____

2) ***Relate***: How does this connect with your life/experiences? Describe a memory, experience or feeling that you've had as a result of this note.

_____

_____

_____

_____

_____

_____

3) ***Release Yourself:*** What actions will you release yourself to take in your life as a result of today's note?

_____

_____

_____

_____

_____

_____

_____

4) Your Own Notes, Questions, Thoughts, Musings

_____

_____

_____

_____

_____

_____

_____

_____

_____

_____

_____

_____

_____

_____

_____

_____

_____

_____

_____

_____

_____

_____

_____

_____

_____

DAY 83

Note 2 Self: "Don't let the fear of success keep you from moving forward."

1) **Reflect**: What do you believe this means? What does it say to you?

_____

_____

_____

_____

_____

_____

_____

2) **Relate**: How does this connect with your life/experiences? Describe a memory, experience or feeling that you've had as a result of this note.

_____

_____

_____

_____

_____

_____

3) **Release Yourself**: What actions will you release yourself to take in your life as a result of today's note?

_____

_____

_____

_____

_____

_____

_____

4) *Your Own Notes, Questions, Thoughts, Musings*

_____

_____

_____

_____

_____

_____

_____

_____

_____

_____

_____

_____

_____

_____

_____

_____

_____

_____

_____

_____

_____

_____

_____

_____

_____

_____

_____

DAY 84

Note 2 Self: "Build your confidence and belief in yourself daily. Pat yourself on the back. Set mini goals and achieve them. You are your best cheering section. Celebrate __YOU__ today!"

1) ***Reflect***: What do you believe this means? What does it say to you?

_____

_____

_____

_____

_____

_____

2) ***Relate***: How does this connect with your life/experiences? Describe a memory, experience or feeling that you've had as a result of this note.

_____

_____

_____

_____

_____

3) ***Release Yourself***: What actions will you release yourself to take in your life as a result of today's note?

_____

_____

_____

_____

_____

_____

_____

_____

4) Your Own Notes, Questions, Thoughts, Musings

_____

_____

_____

_____

_____

_____

_____

_____

_____

_____

_____

_____

_____

_____

_____

_____

_____

_____

_____

_____

_____

_____

_____

_____

_____

DAY 85

Note 2 Self: *"Live your life as if you were able to come back in time and change the things you didn't like. Head off future regrets by the actions you take today."*

1) ***Reflect***: What do you believe this means? What does it say to you?

_____
_____
_____
_____
_____
_____

2) ***Relate***: How does this connect with your life/experiences? Describe a memory, experience or feeling that you've had as a result of this note.

_____
_____
_____
_____
_____

3) ***Release Yourself***: What actions will you release yourself to take in your life as a result of today's note?

_____
_____
_____
_____
_____
_____
_____
_____

4) *Your Own Notes, Questions, Thoughts, Musings*

_____

_____

_____

_____

_____

_____

_____

_____

_____

_____

_____

_____

_____

_____

_____

_____

_____

_____

_____

_____

_____

_____

_____

_____

DAY 86

Note 2 Self: "You have a passion and a dream. Don't let anyone tell you it can't be realized."

1) **Reflect**: What do you believe this means? What does it say to you?

_____

_____

_____

_____

_____

_____

_____

2) **Relate**: How does this connect with your life/experiences? Describe a memory, experience or feeling that you've had as a result of this note.

_____

_____

_____

_____

_____

_____

3) **Release Yourself**: What actions will you release yourself to take in your life as a result of today's note?

_____

_____

_____

_____

_____

_____

_____

4) *Your Own Notes, Questions, Thoughts, Musings*

_____

_____

_____

_____

_____

_____

_____

_____

_____

_____

_____

_____

_____

_____

_____

_____

_____

_____

_____

_____

_____

_____

_____

_____

_____

DAY 87

Note 2 Self: *"If it's not fueling your passion; in line with your purpose or building your legacy; why are you doing it?."*

1) **Reflect**: What do you believe this means? What does it say to you?

_____
_____
_____
_____
_____
_____
_____

2) **Relate**: How does this connect with your life/experiences? Describe a memory, experience or feeling that you've had as a result of this note.

_____
_____
_____
_____
_____
_____

3) **Release Yourself**: What actions will you release yourself to take in your life as a result of today's note?

_____
_____
_____
_____
_____
_____
_____

4) Your Own Notes, Questions, Thoughts, Musings

_____

_____

_____

_____

_____

_____

_____

_____

_____

_____

_____

_____

_____

_____

_____

_____

_____

_____

_____

_____

_____

_____

_____

_____

DAY 88

Note 2 Self: "You are NOT powerless. Embrace your power. Recognize it. Accept it. Exercise it."

1) **Reflect**: What do you believe this means? What does it say to you?

_____
_____
_____
_____
_____
_____
_____

2) **Relate**: How does this connect with your life/experiences? Describe a memory, experience or feeling that you've had as a result of this note.

_____
_____
_____
_____
_____
_____

3) **Release Yourself**: What actions will you release yourself to take in your life as a result of today's note?

_____
_____
_____
_____
_____
_____
_____

4) *Your Own Notes, Questions, Thoughts, Musings*

_____

_____

_____

_____

_____

_____

_____

_____

_____

_____

_____

_____

_____

_____

_____

_____

_____

_____

_____

_____

_____

_____

_____

_____

_____

_____

DAY 89

Note 2 Self: "You are the success you hope to become."

1) **Reflect**: What do you believe this means? What does it say to you?

_____

_____

_____

_____

_____

_____

_____

2) **Relate**: How does this connect with your life/experiences? Describe a memory, experience or feeling that you've had as a result of this note.

_____

_____

_____

_____

_____

_____

3) **Release Yourself**: What actions will you release yourself to take in your life as a result of today's note?

_____

_____

_____

_____

_____

_____

_____

4) *Your Own Notes, Questions, Thoughts, Musings*

_____

_____

_____

_____

_____

_____

_____

_____

_____

_____

_____

_____

_____

_____

_____

_____

_____

_____

_____

_____

_____

_____

_____

_____

DAY 90

Note 2 Self: "You have the power to accept what is; acknowledge what has been and to create what will be for you in your life."

1) ***Reflect***: What do you believe this means? What does it say to you?

_____

_____

_____

_____

_____

_____

_____

2) ***Relate***: How does this connect with your life/experiences? Describe a memory, experience or feeling that you've had as a result of this note.

_____

_____

_____

_____

_____

3) ***Release Yourself***: What actions will you release yourself to take in your life as a result of today's note?

_____

_____

_____

_____

_____

_____

_____

4) *Your Own Notes, Questions, Thoughts, Musings*

_____
_____
_____
_____
_____
_____
_____
_____
_____
_____
_____
_____
_____
_____
_____
_____
_____
_____
_____
_____
_____
_____
_____
_____
_____
_____
_____
_____
_____
_____

Congratulations!

Volume 1 of "Note 2 Self" is complete!

You have undertaken a journey to know and understand yourself more fully and in the process, to become a better "you".

Hopefully the past 90 days have inspired you, enlightened you and motivated you.

If you would like to continue the conversation, or to participate in The Release Yourself Series™ of The KARS Paperback Coaching Program™, visit our website at www.karsgroup.com for additional books in the series.

Take the time each day to make yourself better than you were the day before!

KEISHA A. RIVERS-SHORTY

ABOUT THE AUTHOR

Keisha A. Rivers-Shorty

I have many "labels".

I am a coach, teacher, speaker and consultant. I am an entrepreneur, adjunct instructor, grant writer and founder of The KARS Group, LTD and The KARS Institute of Learning and Collaboration.

But most of all I am a life-learner and a journey(wo)man.

I do what I do because at my core I am a teacher and I believe in helping others to have that "ah-ha" moment when something becomes clear for them and they have the excitement and confidence to use their new understanding in new ways.

My passion comes from wanting to see and create that moment. My purpose comes from a desire to see everyone experience it throughout their lives. I want to build a legacy where my "students" pass along their knowledge to others so that the ripple of my single touch spreads far and wide.

Made in the USA
Lexington, KY
30 March 2017